At This Table

by

Raphael Block

Books by Raphael Block
Songs From a Small Universe (2009)
Spangling Darkness (2014)
Strings of Shining Silence (2017)

Spangling Darkness, Strings of Shining Silence,
and *At This Table* are all freely available as
recordings at http://www.raphaelblock.com

Cover art and design by Judyth Greenburgh

Poetic Matrix Press
www.poeticmatrix.com

At This Table

Preface

I look back at the deep sighs expressed in these poems, sighs of love and longing that we share in the same spirit breath. My short sojourn here, embraced by this great, generous being Earth, asks of me to "give back one speck, one jot, of all / you pour into these marrowed bones" (from *Meeting Light*, in this book). Beauty is one way of doing this, as are tending to plants, caring for animals, and participating in our own communities. There is no limit to the power we can express in our lives on a daily basis. As Mother Theresa said, "Small things with great love. The moment we offer them to (Spirit), they become infinite."

May these verses be a source of surprise, discovery, and uplift for you. Please feel free to share them in whatever way comes most naturally to you, be it song, dance, drawing, reciting, quilting, posting, or any other form.

Acknowledgments

Thank you, Terry Ehret, for editing all my books! And thank you for modeling so beautifully how to live and give to the communities you serve. Thank you, Caroline Miller, for copyediting once again. Thank you, Nan Hopkin, for your behind-the-scenes feedback and for your sensitive and acute observations. Thank you, Carol Griffin, for all your loving support and for working with me on *The Passion of Yusuf (Joseph) and Zulaikha*. Thank you, Tim Ray, for recording my two books, *Strings of Shining Silence* and *At This Table*. Thank you, John Maas, for your choral compositions of *October Butterfly* and *Pink Lilies*. And thank you, John Peterson, for your choice of fonts to complement the general tone of the poems, and for publishing my last three books!

Deep gratitude to my Sufi teachers, Mrs. Tweedie and Llewellyn Vaughan-Lee, for casting your light and love.

I would like to acknowledge *Birdland Journal* for publishing *Meeting Light* (Fall 2018); *The California Quarterly* for publishing *Night*

(Fall 2018, Vol.44, Number 3)); *Stealing Fire* and *Unlikely and Least* (Summer 2019, Vol. 45, Number 2); and Larry Robinson for sending out some of these pieces on his *e-Poem-a-Day*.

I would also like to express my delight with Judyth Greenburgh's cover design, and for her flexibility and willingness to go that extra mile.

Contents

Preface
Acknowledgments
Contents

At This Table

This Snail

This Table

Into Your Arms

Let the Wind

Open Moment

The Passion of Yusuf (Joseph) and Zulaikha

Heart Throne

Poems and Songs by Raphael Block
Composed for Choir by John Maas

About the Author

At This Table

This Snail

Now a window
of slowness
opens

so this snail
can return
to itself
and its true
home.

This Table

This Table

How amazing is this day!
    The spider's web casts its shadow
play, lilies sing in sprays,
    redwoods and broad oaks hold sway.
Ripe berries for beaks and lips,
    patches of white lace—all set
on this delicate plate. We,
    at your table, but guests.

unlikely and least
after e e cummings

when faces called flowers come out rain-
splashing all rainbow bands but green
and *treely* buds whisper crimson again
hills come alive skipping echoes
hearts and wings fast flutter with spring

scent plum blossom reels
the naked come clothed and the clothed
shyly naked, for all is giddy
and skyless, tumbling in vastness and outness
earth's belly first cries spring

while those under the willow broken
cry out—their ringing passion
midwifing—crocus shoots rise
felt yet unseen in faces
unlikely and least

Summer Winds

High summer winds gust and blow
    reddening apples, plums, bow and
show themselves in these shaping
    shimmers. A streaming rush sounds as
a troop of white clouds straddles
    the hill, while up in the redwood
cluster, high-pitched trills bound and
    flutter over yellowing grasses.

A swell of molecules cascades.
    Once more all is fro and to, to
and fro, playful limbs sway. Yet
    silence reigns—not reins the vigorous
motion in, not at all, but
    the springboard for birds' commotion,
whistling trees, a soaring vulture,
    and my rustling heart—now still.

Fingerling

Fingerling of
   blossoming pine
I would
  never have
noticed you so
  high on a branch

child and parent
  of seventy feet
arms spiraling
  outward and upward
in perpetual
  dance

fallen
  from your nest
you lie—
  creamy-yellow clusters
between green
  soft needles shine

from brown
    overlapping cones
all wrapped in
    wafting perfume—
I name you
    thousand blessings.

Unsung Songs

A thousand branches vault
    into the bird-bound blue, while
feathered darkly on gnarly limbs
    my unsung songs roost unseen.
I lean closer, closer
    to hear them croon.

Loops of vibrant singing
    sweep as bright-eyed
robin greets each branch and twig
    before springing nimble.

Lilting notes propel
    crocus shoots past snow
and rock, their bulbs
    surviving mole and worm.
Daffodils burst inside and
    shining chime.

Love reels and spirals
    to my roots—wills me keen
my sorrow, moan my pain,
    woo those hymns snowed
under shame to take wing
    in circling flight.

The Hum

Wings awhir,
   long curved beak
      lavishes loving care
         on each purple bell.

Salvia, in turn,
   opens a few florets
      for her guests.

Back and forth darts
   a green-winged gleam,
      zooms up for a rest
         in silver birch.

A quick dive
   into open flowers,
      tongue flicking faster
         than eye can follow

gleam flits away
　　for a solitary second
　　　　hummer to weave
　　　　　　its fluttering melody.

Glinting red and green
　　sun-flashing throats—
　　　　feisty foragers
　　　　　　hover on fall feast.

The Lunge

Wind whips across his white body
　　rippling those soft feathers—
waves riding in the nearby bay.
　　His six-inch spear, bound to two
beady eyes and serpentine neck,
　　leads this great question mark
balancing on black stilts.

Poised, intent on hunting along
　　a bank of ice plant by Lucas Wharf
a few feet off the coastal highway,
　　he barely blinks at car alarms and
engine starts, as he stands
　　stretched above hidden holes.

His neck stiffens, begins to snake—
　　a downward lunge, white wings outspread
over a full-grown gopher plucked
　　from its den. He works it
between that razor yellow beak,
　　bringing it closer to his gullet
bit by bit. A quick flick

of his head and that furry body's
   now visible only as muscled
movement down his quavering nape.
   The great bird stands still,
then returns to utter focus
   above the holes nestled
below purple-rayed flowers.

My Mary and Martha
(Luke 10: 38-42)

Call this person, email that one!
Martha watches the items
on a never-ending *To Do* list
slide off the page, like small beads
on a slope or scented vegetable
peelings poured onto the compost
leaving only the basics:
rice, milk and bread.
Everything else can wait,
including my nagging mind.

Mary hears a flock
of upside-down chickadees sing
as they glean insects
off the oak leaves, a pair
of beating dark wings
on a blue body darting among flowers,
a friend's call. My *To Do* list lets go
and we are all the happier. Watering
the garden, responding—all will
happen in their own good time.

A whisper dances inside
drawing me near—
away from the glittering
din of distractions
toward the sweet notes
of Mary's devotions,
while my Martha
cooks soup in the kitchen.

Destiny Tango

This hyacinth fills the room
   with its sweet scent.
     Like a huge fruit
      it leans its head

toward the earth.
   Grown from bulb, crammed
     in a small pot, it seems
      unable to fulfill its goal

to offer pollen, fertilize
   the ground with seed,
     scatter purple petals
      on a breeze

yet it will find a way around
to make its bow both lasting and profound.

The Choicest Plum

The dawning sun hidden in the trees
    spies me standing beside long strands
        of ruby plums, reaching to feel each fruit

one by one, until a glistening orb slips
    into my palm and dripping lips
        under that ripening, radiant one.

Making Porridge

Soak dried apricots to expand
and meet the day; toast oats
to drive out the rancid; add
milk for life's kindness; a dash
of salt for rock-bottom support;
a handful of blueberries—their star-like
openings touching our origins. Peel
an apple for nakedness of soul and bow
to its core, whose seeds of wisdom
can be tapped as needed.

Bring all these to a slow simmer.
Let them bubble and mingle
yielding their goodness.

Sprinkle wheat germ from fields
of brown waves; yogurt to foster
bovine patience. Cradle the bowl—
enjoy its warmth and smells.
Chew caringly to overcome
a lifetime of hurrying.

Choose your own way of making,
and whether it tastes bitter
or sweet, embrace it!

Dusk Alights

When forget-me-nots
   have quieted, and
      all greens blur in

the slow, fading light,
   you may have seen
      the calla lilies shining.

They sail so
   white, their hearts
      sway above

broad leaves,
   yellow pollen fingers
      point upward

grooved tracks
   draw you inward
      to a cusp, where

you hold your breath
   until you hear
      a long, soft sigh.

Meeting Light

Through the windshield, light gleams
on the fields. The light green willow leaves
running along the creeks
seem brighter set

against the just-beginning greening hills
dotted with oaks, cows, sheep,
small clumps of shy-hoofed deer.
All chomp in well-manured pastures
as I, too, stand richly fed.

Vultures wing soundless circles overhead,
a perched hawk, red-tailed, its haunting
call withdrawn, spies smaller prey;
crows rush, gust and clatter
onto walnut limbs to cackle and muster.

I loom with the hunter,
quail with its prey, prattle
with companions until our souls
are full-flush fleshed.

By Walker Creek, a thousand white woolen
eyes crown coyote brush,
dried fennel stalks drop silent seed.
Among these wild ones I flourish and breathe
under sun-fog-rain sway.

Coiling bends round the broadening bay
whose undulating ripples peep between,
lending ease and grace
against the pine-clad ridges, as the scudding sun
plays upon my skin into unseen depths.

Sprawled on the verge, a car-killed deer
awaits its airborne team with sharpened smell
to pick it clean. All seeps, sings, and bounds in me.
Is it the light or the light
that I am soon to leave?

On boughed knees rest old oaks sinking
into softened sod. The turns of seasons watch.
Their path is slowly set, while mine is filled
with urgency to laud and praise

give back one speck, one jot, of all
you pour into these marrowed bones.

Winter Solstice Shine

They have come for fine berries,
                in droves, in lines.
A few flapfuls and gulps
                and off they fly
to sing praise in the oaks,
                firs, and pines.
Drunken whistles echo under
                mauve sunshine,
rusty-orange chests pressed
                on bright red wine.

Into Your Arms

meeting

just a few looks
        and words,
feelings travel
        through air
and our hearts
        lift or drown
in love
        or love's sorrow

all it takes
        is one strike
from the flint
        to spark
each other—

for tinder
        to light
a tenderizing
        fire

October Butterfly

Far-flung butterfly
    fanning yourself on a mound
in a patch of October sun,
    those orange black-dotted
wings have spun and spun
    through summer months.
Is your harvesting done?

Swaying bay branches
    barely hint at your bright
bursts of flight, when
    for turn of speed I
could only glimpse you
    sparely lighting on
some leaf or flower.

Your dark, still center
    as motionless
as the fulcrum

of a fan. One step closer
and you're off again whirling—
    now and now
all that counts.

Pregnant Air

Whipping wind and rain
   hammering and echoing
     in bending trees, clattering
      on skylights, lashing

rooftops and power lines
   with bounteous ease.
     Rhythmically abating,
      like the trough of a wave

before belting onto fence
   and balustrade. Pelting
     decks, a steady rumble
      cascades, charges

pregnant air to spring
   a rush of streams—
     all is flow, all is awe,
      while we shelter from the squall.

Revel in these powers
    that holy earth displays—
        our mountains of denial
            taller than the Himalayas.

Into Your Arms

Upside down among Doug fir cones
swoop gray and white bushtits. So fast
they flit, so high their chatter, and where
can they fly but into your arms
of branch, twig and sky.

A garrulous three on a bare apple
tree sally onto the grassy field,
stir the soil for worms and seeds.
Dazzling blue with orange chests,
back they shoot onto brown limbs
with a flurry and flutter of whistles
and wings. Where will they nest?

And come the spring swallows, where
will we dwell? Crevices, sandbanks, and
walls, under bridges, ledges, in caves,
adobe, thatched and assorted homes, all
in your arms my dearest, my sweet, all
in your arms.

Like flocks of white swans we people
rivers, marshes, ponds—like bald eagles
so high we soar, so hard we fall,
yet always, all ways in your arms,
where can we stray but into your arms.

Vaux Swifts

A trickle of black dots in the distance
swooping here and there for evening fare
swirls into a circling whir,
vanishes, then returns. Twinkling airplane
lights; in the east a full moon mounts.
.

Faster, faster, their carousel swings
around an invisible pole,
thicker, thicker grows this patchwork
of ten thousand wings, with no
hint of their roosting place tonight.

Dark blurs fill the sky with high orbital
trills, breathtaking dives, intent on aerial dance.
A few start to drop into a disused flue,
as thousands on thousands wait
their turn. They swarm swiftly
while a small stream funnels—

bidden by what?—into that black hole.
A sudden scattering—then they burst
into a figure eight, soar into the fading
light, while far lower, a brisk
flow continues to slip into shelter's arms.

In a matter of minutes they bed themselves
with stunning precision. Flutters
of wings and twitters,
    silence—
       they're gone.

One-Eyed

My one-eyed cat licks rainwater in the plant bowl.
She doesn't mind that there's mud in the bottom.
Her paws scuttle across the wet deck

while all beyond hides under a white drape.
One-eyed, two-eyed, or blind, stillness
as thickly spread as homemade jam.

Cold Rain and Winds

A shroud of morning mist
  blankets the hills and dips.
    Threads of crystal-clear drops
      clothe each bare twig.

The bay tree sways beside
  a towering eucalyptus.
    Invisible strands pull
      here and there.

Ah, to be content, bathed
  by splash of rain—
    when going anywhere
      for the going to remain

at peace, for the somewhere
  to arrive before
    these open portals
      undisturbed by driving winds.

Summer Storm

Sky flashes. Rolling banks
of sonic waves crack and echo
through ceiling rafters.

This is no fight among raccoons
with spine-tingling, guttural cries,
or a stag chased down by
a roar, teeth and claws
closing in for the kill.

This is no artillery duel or
the ricochet of big gun barrels raining
destruction on the fields.

This is just ancient, sheer terror—
light and thunder releasing
summer rain, pent-up energies,
locked-up body memories.

Let it strike the dark, sizzling sky,
let it deafen the ear with deep
bounding bass, whether we
cower or dance

or bow down
to the thirsting earth,
our pores open
to creation's sparks.

Mount Shasta

Smell of late-summer grass and horses.
Reddish-brown dock seeds and yellowing weeds
outcrop the rocks. Low pine-clad hills, a sweet
singing in the cool breeze. The herd's shadows
ripple across the field in a slow wave.
Between nibbles of grass, long, elegant necks
rise below a full moon. High above
towers snow-capped Shasta.

Love Notes

She used to leave me notes:
　　"I'm on a walk,"
"Gone to meet a friend,"
　　but no longer.

Sunlight on the horizon
　　the song of a robin
a companion's wise words;
　　"Ask for what you need.
　　　　That, too, is sacred."

Queen Anne's lace dotting
　　the landscape, scent
of summer peach—
　　all sound your name

even as my overcast heart
　　wails like a cat for
the subtle manna that fills
　　this frame, and without notice
　　　　empties it again.

Judas Tree

Hundreds of bright brown pods,
like flocks roosting on wires,
rustle among round
yellow-veined leaves,
below high woolen clouds
of early fall.

Schoolkids weighed by
backpacks trudge home. Parents
weighted by worries—
their eyes on the concrete.

Do we dare see—
do we dare be—
this stark beauty
all about?

Clear Silhouettes

Let go the torments of your mind
beside a tree
              your aches and pains
embrace it as a friend who gives
you ease

suddenly double wings flit
              into the canopy
its silhouetted leaves
              leap out
clear as your soul itself

with each breath the day
meets you afresh

Bouquet

What can you say
when out of the blue
a girl hands
you a red poppy
and a dandelion
she had plucked for herself?

You have been given
no less than the sun
and Jupiter
for companions.

You were plodding uphill
under an old load
and whoosh! Now it's flown
and you're soaring.

Purple wings, two tipped
with white splash,
imprint on

the poppy's petals—
a smattering of yellow pollen
dots a silky red expanse.

Did the poppy stalk
bend when she slipped
its end inside
the hollow
dandelion stem
making a perfect bouquet?

Ah, *dents-de-lion,*
young lioness,
your smile entrances.

Let the Wind

Pink Lilies

When they first appear
    tall, trumpeting summer,
naked of leaf, yet full
    of intoxicating scent,
messengers springing
    from the bulbous earth
peering through long grass
    and beds, you wish they
would last forever, you wish
    they would last forever,
knowing your own
    period of grace is short,
like theirs, though we mark ours
    with more seasons.

They will resurrect next year
    while we? The mystery blows
far ahead. Only inner knowing
    might catch a glimpse of pink
and deeper pink
    swaying on a stem.

He Comes to Taste

He comes to taste
    late apples still hanging
        in November, but my
            entry startles him.

Swerving,
    his noble antlers
        turn, gauging
            which route to take.

His gait, once limber,
    tells of old injuries.
        Across the neighbor's line
            he stumbles and quickens

following the still-dry
    gully out of sight
        then slowly trots
            into the tall meadow

following a doe.
    More dark coats flicker
        among the tawny stalks;
            cars press on their way.

A vulture wheels
    over the scene
        as now and then
        an oak leaf tumbles
      spiraling in the cool
afternoon breeze.

Dancing Lightly

For Jenya (1952 - 2013)

a breath of cloud
 dye-flushed sky
turning leaves cool air
 on my cheeks
this—the last time
 I sense the earth—now
as freshly
 as the first

leaves twist whirl
 while I spin
  earthward
clouds shift—each
 moment my eyes'
  witness is borne
   by others' eyes
  my plucked chords
echo in others' feet

my pulsing warmth
    quickens hearts
        as the wind picks up
   and leaves begin
to wheel   to dance.

Squall

The winds that will be howling at all hours
And are up-gathered now like sleeping flowers;
For this, for everything we are out of tune...
William Wordsworth

Oak florets, like dangling earrings
of tiny purple grapes,
waver in the breeze.
They fear we overlook the miracle
of their birth and spirit
that inhabits them from root to tip.

A wave hovers over valleys
and redwood ridges.
It sounds through the crow's dark calls,
crashes on deaf bones.

By god,
the rocks live more soulfully than we!
Glorious
wavelengths beaming across the cosmos.

I Take Drugs for Kicks

I don't just mean my daily round
of vitamins and pills.
What I take gives me
a mood-and-mind altered state—
I become what I see—
golden-crowned sparrows

hopping in hedges, splashes
and scents of fresh mint and
sweet pea. I take off
out the door
one foot after the other
for my fresh-air fix.

Recovery

Basking in warmth
   comes the autumn sun
not striding, or panting
   or dallying or driven
or chasing shadows,
   it effortlessly follows its path
and I, one ray,
   bend to its blessing—
align my own
   orbit with those
circling this heavenly
   and earthly body.

A Stitch in Time

Two pairs of flashing forceps crisscross
the river of my eye. The egrets dive,
beaks click-clacking, and rise
toward the light. Again and again

they dip, twisting and turning—
a tickle of thread. Up they fly
with the catch back to the surgeon's
hands. The suture's done!

Let the Wind

Granted sight again, I reel
   among reveling leaves. The bay
      and eucalyptus swing their limbs
         while a half-naked oak pirouettes.

A thorny, dark-branched plum leans
   into a paper birch rocking and
      shaking a few last handfuls of golden
         flutters among its dangling cones.

Let the wind do its work, let
   the wind do its work, strip
      and spin me, too,
         through and through.

By the Hospital Pharmacy

They couldn't be birds! It was only a quilt of soft-scored, undulating lines flowing on a sky of light pink, circling into blues. Somewhere within the striped border and flowered-ribbon edge, four-inch squares appear fluttering diagonally. Within each square, two triangles meet, flapping upward, upward. One red, bearing white-leafed circles, one blue with small red stars. One checkered triangle, paired with a wing of green and blue flowers, another of orange trellises and white-petaled sets.

Stand back, stand back! The flock is taking off. Only they know their destination— as my heart lifts off with them.

Reflections

White and gray cupped
  willow buds held
    in golden goblets
      like pollen caterpillars

borne on the same twig—
  faint spring scent ebbs and
    rises with evening song—
      red-winged blackbirds

and grand-voiced small birds
  chorus by the banks
    of furrowed waters spattered
      with showers, overhanging

branches, a mound of cloud,
  reflect back all there is.

Each Moment That I Am Fine-Tuned

through my breath, slowed thinking
and feeling step, the mountain of ease
and grace grows larger

the chasm of sorrow and joy deeper,
sheer heights of unscaled gratitude
echo louder

up and down a thundering canyon
that won't dry out
in harshest summer.

This stone begins to roll, speeds up,
meets others, triggers an avalanche
of peace.

Matinée

Cirrus clouds, once ocean bound,
  come racing in. This one's a raccoon,
piercing eyes, dark mask,
  before breaking into wisps so thin.
Here comes a giant-eyed mermaid,
  tail whipping. Skulls sail, monsters dive—
whatever you wish!

A fluffy, white poodle skates by
  and dissolves. Thick layers slide
and chassé, chased by waves riding
  on waves, spirit devas, and pirates
no longer moored or marooned, sally
  over these hills, bringing drama,
planks, pranks, and summer cool.

The pot of creation so lightly stirred—
  simple ingredients, sun, water, air.
Here bounds a gorilla, ahhhh!
  swallowed by a horrible glob.
Spinning together
  they've become a cloud Buddha!

A sad-eyed troll has taken its toll.
   A genie asleep on its back wakes up
as an elephant! And a big-nosed pronghorn
   is grinning along. Here they all play
on the local outdoor screen.
   Don't miss them, don't miss them,
it's a one-time only release!
hem, it's a one-time-only release!

She Comes to Savor

A young doe on
  frosty ground pulls on
    the juicy turf growing
      along the leach lines.

Eyes and ears ever alert
  she bends to chew—raising
    her elongated neck
    while oval ears turn.

Her white rump, face,
  and tufts match the hoarfrost,
    her darkened coat
      the color of a bare oak.

She makes her way along
  the meadow slope towards
    the neighbor's fence line,
      vanishing in the pasture.

As the sun touches
    the eucalyptus top,
I spy her some two hundred
    yards downhill,
back and neck arching
    down and up again.

Among the evergreens
    clothing these hills,
bare poplars and red gums
    flame. A siren sounds
on the winding highway—
    all falls still.

The Irish Fiddler

For fiddler Martin Hayes and guitarist
Dennis Cahill

His feet beat quarter notes and measures
like horses cantering up a bridleway
while his bow points to the mountains—
a steady uphill climb along running brooks
heather-purple rocks, straggling trees

rooted tenaciously. For the descent,
the team picks up pace past scree
slopes, green vales, smell of sweet hay
drawing them faster, faster.

The fiddler's torso twists and bobs, turning
the trot into a gallop. At the swish of swell
and waves, the driving guitar picks up the reins.
The team is free—to leave the path,
take off beyond the peaks, beyond the cloud.

Threaded droplets of sound boundlessly
cascade in waterfall bursts until we're taken
over that ledge. Then there is no waterfall—
no water. We land outdistanced by ourselves.

Stealing Fire

Paper and thin apple twigs catch the first match.
Crow fans his wings, cackles and caws, letting
everyone know what I've stolen.
I add fatter sticks.

But fire won't be rushed.
I eye the whispering tongues.
Next, some pine and eucalyptus—
welcome heat springs.

Then the first log. A mad reel begins
as flickering flames spiral,
lick and fly. Crow is stoked,
laughing with each crackle

that wildly leaps and jigs
and once dead, ends up like his black coat.
The fire must be fed, the fire must be fed,
crow taunts. And what of our own starving gods?

Open Moment

House Finch

Perched on a cart, flash
    your orange-red forehead
and chest, while from your
    stubby bill sounds
a gorgeous melody.

You swoop to earth and trill,
    pecking in the thick
of a rosemary hedge—
    just a few feet from
the highway's roar.

In the middle of April
    showers, others take up
the song—some let
    their hearts carry
them home.

And I Bow Low

i hear the deep rumble of thunder,
winter rain, a mighty clap

as wild winds chase around
the canopies until all let go

moss clumps on the oak's bark
while overnight, long-stemmed toadstools

sprout in moist mosaic warmth, a narcissus
feigns spring with heady perfume

forget-me-nots rise beneath unfurling
leaves, like newborn souls

the moth and butterfly slip out
of their spiral-wrapped homes

dark-eyed juncos splash in puddles,
ruffle my reflections and i bow low

my love's whisper—is it fluting
through a sparrow's song or borne
on that hovering hawk's wings?

The Promise

Who will go on this journey
with me? Who will go?

There's no promise
of money, good health,
fame or success.
Who will
go? Who?

Through murderous
shadows, writhing
snakes, giants,
tormented thieves,
your prisoners
unleashed, loss
of purse and friends.
Who will go, who will still go?

Through dark nights
awake
the screech

of a barn owl
starting its beat—
you its prey.

Beaten and broken
until you give up—
when first light
finds its way.
Who will go
with me? Who will?

To meet the glow
of your dreams—
a sunrise
inside—
the melting of fear

first song
hushed wings
of each fresh
heart day.

Who will go with me?
Who will go?

In the Bhav ("Stream of Love")

With thanks to Bhavani Judith
Tucker for her friendship, and lyrics
for "The Heart Knows the Way."

The heart knows the way...
Let it whisper all its secrets...
What is searing you today...
will cast diamonds on the altar of the heart...

blue eyes reflect
        blue translucent light
        now open now shut
            beneath graying curls,
    curled strumming fingers
play thundercloud blue

earth brown guitar,
inset Durga mother of pearls,
millennia of her Krishna core
        to fine-tune Bhavani's songs—
quicken
        hearten

ignite
  vault deep
  and high
  each note lived
  and coursing
through

spilling into
words and sounds
    Hebrew English Sanskrit—
in the *Bhav*—
  all her vibrations torch
  my naked soul's urge.

The heart knows the way...
  Let it whisper all its secrets...
  What is searing you today...
  will cast diamonds on the altar of the heart...

The Hanging Gardens

Beside the long birch,
    golden yellow trailings
and a reddish-orange maple,
    a wooden stairwell leads
to a small stoop.
    Here, I sense—through
open slatted blinds—the fabled
    Babylonian Gardens.

Leaves spill in bunches
    still against a thick-white
early-morning curtain.
    Faint sounds of the well
and highway rumble
    as my pulsing heart
skips beats in its coop.

Clap and Sing!
After Kabir

The honeybee sings as it hovers
    from blossom to blossom,
the tiny forget-me-not feels
        as giving as the wide daisy,
the butterfly drinking nectar
    claps its wings in delight.

Raphael, you worry about
    a pimple here, a scar there—
indignities of the body.
    Rejoice you're able
to witness such joy
    and bear what needs be.

The Mound

So, I cover myself with busyness, anything
to paper over the cracks of pain, the call
from the hive. My sweetness lies
in joking asides and fishing for companions
whose fear-hidden eyes won't look
past the smoke screen masking our view
through the window panes.

Yellow jackets fiercely contest my half-baked
reflections. Now and then, I catch a rupture
in my laughter, a fish bone momentarily snagged
in a gullet. Through the tides of exhausted nights
my mind and body churn. In their wake
of white-capped hopes, only the gulls give voice
shrieking and plunging.

The days and months pitch and plummet
in the wind. My bones, grown hollow,
drip with the fat of half-digested events.
My smile bares itself. My sunken eyes suffer
the nobility of age behind manicured looks
and hunger unabated.

In my sleep, the sound of swarming wakes.
The bees have built an earthen mound
whose insides are thickly crusted with honey.
How I long for their sweet song!
With my bare hands I tear at its walls
to touch that clotted substance,
to smear it over my mouth and tongue,
hair, chest, legs, and arms.

For All Things

Jewels of searing red-
   and amber-lacquered leaves
gold rippling on the waves
   silver moonlit beams
the tidal breath
   your honeyed touch
melons' steeped perfume
   all things precious to which
we may lay no claim

The crow's caw riding on the wind
   the quail's high-pitched laugh
a thrush's song, lavender's
   scent in winter's spring,
for the way life walks through us
   the rich tones of your voice
evening's hush,
   all things precious
we simply cannot claim.

A burst of blinding rays
   the deep pools of your eyes

a wing's pulse inside
　　the doe with her two fawns
stock still, crinkly frost
　　sapping the old
warm winter grain
　　and all things precious to which
we may lay no claim.

Redwood woven roots
　　coho salmon leaps
for all that moves
　　the hummingbird's flashing flame
a heart of wax
　　cocoons wrapped in spring
your ever-playful spark
　　all things precious
we simply cannot claim.

The Queen

When the piping of the queen
    does start, the young queens in their cells
cannot resist the call, and gently
    piping back, the queen unsheathes her
sword, and stabs through each
    sealed door until their song is heard
no more. A silence falls across the
    hive before the bees recoil.
Only One will rule, only one
    Will rules—rings throughout the combs
and echoes round and round the walls.

Keening Hawk

I hear your cry carrying
across the valley. I
can't see you, yet
your call touches
something so deep—
a half-remembered chord.

Your pitch rises in
urgent flight as you
land in a distant pine.
Your cries settle, but
not mine, stirred to some
unnameable sorrow.

Ah, it's the pain of
love—keen, alive, divine!

Open Moment

There comes a moment
when the tree's orange glow
outweighs its yellow-green
large oval leaves
and it hurts
to face them
because the sweet longing
culled from my chest
the slow burning
of a subtle blaze
spreads and spreads

Takeover

Fog rolls in, cloaking
   these valleys and hills.
It swoops like a cast
      of vultures who've
scented the kill.

I've grown so tired
      of this cover story
that scrapes by on carrion—
      my mind's reruns
of stale drama clips
      my nagging rotting lists

I need you to take over.
      I want you to swoop in.

Knock-Kneed

Fighting for each
captured breath
I stop
to rest,
my heart
spellbound by
two slugs
twined in a
double helix
on a red brick
wall—

bubbling froth
while they coil
in unbroken
embrace
before this
too-human
clay.

No words
can map
the ripples that
cosmic act
spawned
for months
fermenting inside
until it forced
me knock-kneed
to your
door.

The Nourishing Bird of Longing

A huge bird of turquoise greens
                        and blues lifts off.
Is she a phoenix rising or is she bent on flying
                        into the licking flames?
Not for her the shy, distant circling
                        of the sun, not for her
                        the hesitancy of fear
but the clear intent in every muscled fiber
                        beating in her body
to follow her sharp beak and lucid eye
                        into those molten tongues
that race toward her at ever greater speed
                        until her cry
                        fuses with the blaze.

The Passion of Yusuf (Joseph) and Zulaikha

The Passion of Yusuf (Joseph)
and Zulaikha
Inspired by Jami's story, *Yusuf and Zulaikha*
and Rumi's poem, *The Phrasing Must Change*

Chorus

Hear this tale of tears and love!
Yusuf, the dreamer, favorite
of Jacob's sons, now a slave
of Potiphar, Egypt's Grand Vizier.
Zulaikha, Potiphar's wife,
while only still a teen, struck
by visions of overwhelming
love—was it Yusuf? She follows
her dreams through thick and thin,
she follows her dream through years.

Zulaikha

I see him every day, feel his gentle presence,
his changing expressions—amused lines
dancing 'round the corners of his mouth,
his knotted brow—I want to be the answer
to his questions—his upright shoulders,

commanding air, his face as if backlit
by the sun. Through those eyes
unbearable brightness flares.

I long for you, Yusuf, although you are
my husband's slave. "Yusuf, have the grapes
ripened in the vineyard?" "Yusuf, how do you
rate the new Cook?" "It's time we took
inventory, Yusuf." So, I pester you, just to be near.

Oh, why did I pull you into my room,
bare my bosom, tear at your shirt?
Why did I cry out as you turned away,
and when the guards came, blame you?
Oh, my shame at your leaving! Now—
in Pharaoh's jail—instead of in my arms!

Chorus

Oh woe, oh woe! Yusuf locked
in darkness again. Twenty years ago
his brothers threw him down a pit
and sold him for a pittance
into slavery, yes, into slavery.

Yusuf

I cried and cried with the pain
of my brothers' betrayal.
How could all ten of them
have lied to our father?

My face now against cold earth floor,
a rope cutting into my wrists, I twist
over until my feet reach an iron door—
muffled groans down distant corridors.

The night is long. Oh, Zulaikha!
I ache to be near you. My yearning
crashes like a wave. I can't help
but forgive you.

Zulaikha

Yusuf—lost to me.
I'll meet with the warden, ask or bribe him
to treat my love with care, find out
how he fares, what hope for release.

Yusuf

Prisoners and guards come with their worries
and raveled dreams. Sometimes,
they leave a little lighter.

I hear the clacking of storks in the reeds.
I dream of my father still grieving. I long
for you, Zulaikha—your musk-scented hair,
flashing eyes, your long fingers scrolling
down lists, your hands that beckoned,
and sometimes brushed against my arm.
Your laughter of poppy-full fields.

Zulaikha

Yusuf visited in my dream last night.
He kneels and gives me a spray
of spring narcissus. Such tenderness
sweeps over me. I surrender
to this hopeless love.

Chorus

Zulaikah has wept for many a year.
Her husband, Potiphar, passed on.

Yusuf still serves his time.
How will Providence untwine?
How will Providence untwine?

Yusuf

Two of Pharaoh's servants turn up, fallen
out of favor, with drooping heads
and fear-weary eyes. The Cupbearer tells
me his dream, "I see a vine, and on the vine
three branches. As soon as it buds
it blossoms, and the clusters ripen
into grapes." Feeling the dream's texture,
hue and scent, I say, "Within three days,
Pharaoh will restore you to the Court."

Then the Chief Baker relates,
"On my head three baskets of bread. In
the top basket all kinds of baked goods
for Pharaoh but the birds devour them."
I answer, "Within three days you'll be hung
on a tree and birds will peck at your flesh."

Zulaikha

My hair's turned white, my eyes pale gray
from crying night and day. But when

I breathe your name, the bitter tastes sweet.
I pray and pray just to touch you, Love.

Chorus

Pharaoh commands your presence!
Make haste and dress, make haste and dress!

Yusuf

In the middle of a moonless night, I'm ushered
in, to piercing eyes. "My Cupbearer tells me
you understand dreams." Pharaoh unburdens
his weight-crushed breast. I hear
the raucous cries and beat of harsh wings—
I've caught the thread. "Your Highness,
seven years of bounty will be followed
by seven years of famine." Pharaoh stares,
"What can I do?" "Build granaries throughout
the land. Decree one fifth of each harvest
be kept back, so none may lack."
Pharaoh nods, leans forward, slips
his signet ring onto my hand.

Chorus

Within an hour Yusuf's fate has swung
from prisoner to second highest
in the land, second highest in the land!

Zulaikha

I've heard the news!
He rides the Pharaoh's chariot
through the streets today!
I'll throw myself on his mercy.

Yusuf

Can it be? Silver-haired and bowing
in the street? Zulaikha, look at me!
Life has burned and emptied us—we see
beyond our youth. Come to me, at last!

Zulaikha

My heart tilts toward you,
pole of my becoming.

Unveiled, our love
reveals worlds.

Like the narcissus in bloom,
I offer my sweet scent.

Once you were my secret lover.
Now, in every sound
your footstep nears.

Chorus

United to Source, their love shines
and grows, flooding over the banks
of the Nile. Although the famine
hits hard, no one is left in want.
No one is left in want.

---

[1] Jami: Yusuf and Zulaikha, edited and translated by
D. Pendlebury (London, The Octagon Press, 1980). Jami,
a Persian mystic (1414 – 1492).
[2] The Essential Rumi, translations by Coleman Barks
with John Moyne (HarperSanFrancisco, 1995).
Jelaluddin Rumi (1207 – 1273).

Heart Throne

Night

After Edna St. Vincent Millay

Night is my sister, and how deep in love
with shadows, clouds, and stars so deep I am.
Though these flaming worlds shine by day,
who stops to acclaim their uncanny ways?

When the first bat flits with alarming
aplomb, announcing that night, my sister,
has come and the blossoming moon floats
into the sky, my sister sets the stage

for the cricket tide, the skulking cat,
Hecate's owl, a singed moth still searching
for the light, a choir of prayers
in full flight. Shadows over-arch and merge.

And though it is chilly, I will gladly
tarry with my many-faced sister, night.

Heart Throne

I lost an eye—what
a relief. Fungus kept
creeping back into my orb
but now no more!

I lost a dear friend within
two weeks—his spirit
soars, though his family
flounders in their grief.

From behind, two sharp-clawed
paws rip open
my chest—my life force
flees in bloody rivulets.

By the banks I sit,
an emptied shell.
One eye takes in all this
terrible magnificence—

fiery leaves swirling
in waters which fall
and flood beyond
my will—

doors flung
open to my throne,
let in lynx, fox, and
you, my friend.

A Sight Divine

A sea of sunny faces greets me—
    they gently wave, familiar friends
        rise once again for the pleasure
            of murmuring, winged creatures—

each petal a ray like you or me,
    each golden pollen center a heart
        like mine or yours, arrayed
            in unpretentious glory

unafraid, open to—breeze, rain,
    the mower's blade. They'll spring
        again to heap their blessings
            on another timeless day.

These Vast Bareheaded Cleaners

Spiraling high on valley thermals, their wings occasionally beat, bringing them closer, closer to circle above the meadow. Familiar black and silvery white undersides lilt and shift, beaks following a scent. One swoops down, lands, bounces a few paces to bury its head in a fresh-struck doe at the road's edge. Two more hop to the carcass to begin the kettle's meal. More settle on power lines nearby to wait their turn. Not a scrap wasted, they take their fill. Others dive in, these sharp-beaked, acid-strong earth cleaners, until engorged dusk and darkness drive them to silent roost.

Morning comes afresh to fan outspread wings above the fog straddling a barely living-dying oak, reaching for the heat of the oncoming sun. Our sister, Death, is bountiful—what mercy she shows her creatures! Our bodies, the first and last nourishment we receive and give to this beloved Earth.

The Great Fisher

This urge to cast for words—
my soul's need to squeeze,
coax, trick, coerce,
to sculpt and shape as I
am shaped, to tender
in cupped hands my common
senses in single witness
on breaths that pulse and beat.

Buoyed by joy
of red-headed vultures
meeting on a swirl of air
a soaring red-tailed hawk
over fields and woods of oak,
bay, pine, madrone—
spiraling silence.

Buoyed by sorrow and regret
for my bumbling ways,

rapt in sheet-splashing rain
as inside heat surges
and burns. Pained by the fall
of trees, and friends—that
unending longing drumming
through arteries and veins.

These are mine to sing
from the depths of the sea
for the shoaling fish
while the oyster pearls.

Prayer for Light

Hear the rustle of fall
in the oaks' dull yellowing
leaves   their downward drift—
see some caught in the firethorn's
orange-red berry cascades   soft-scented
needles litter the ground
a half moon watches over
as the sunlight fades

birds grow more silent
pines more still   dogs pick up
each other's barking while the crawl
of late-summer traffic snakes
along the crest   a fawn bounds
into the apple orchard   all
will have their fill   even us
trussed by the terrible heat we bring

bats flicker among the twilit
trees   ancient grasses sway
as the crickets' echoing song
strikes up this darkest night

The Hawk and the Mockingbird

a red-shouldered hawk
   razor sharp eye and claws
      perched in shade
    silently swoops
baring its orange neck and breast

and with a thrust of wings
   lands in a nearby oak
      where its hooked beak
    plucks out entrails
and swallows them length by length

downhill I hear a mockingbird's refrain
   am I not contained in everything!
      so sing your praises
    sing your pain
for I am your friend

An Underground Stream
After Rilke

An underground stream leads my life's movements
sometimes into torrents and sometimes
into quiet whirls. "I'm in control," I say
watching the surface trickle of tumbling
pebbles and darting fish.

        If I were shown
the thinning oaks, piles of fruit, rotting limbs
and crumbling rocks on the farther shore
and told, "You made these," could I take in
the poverty of my vision?

        How
this Earth and the planets suffer us.

Gift

This wooden bowl given by a friend
    sits on a window sill beside my desk
still filled with the see-through
    ribbons that wrapped the gift.

Its rounded form and lip
    resemble her open face
lit by the many-sided expressions
    of her oh so visible states!

Although our ways seldom meet
    and yes, I own to some regrets,
her light touch and humor
    top this bowl to the brim,
and splashes of laughter
    replenish its shape.

Herringbone Round

Herringbone stripes set against a black skin almost cover one side of my nakedness. I'm sculpted and shaped, sometimes gnawed, often bitten, so I'm always growing smaller. Do I gladly give myself to all comers? I sigh, remembering the one who molded me from sheep's milk into a round protected on all sides by a waxy skin.

In my veins run memories of the flock grazing on a hillside—fresh smells of clover, daisies, dandelions—of the hands that squeezed me out of a mammal's warm udders. It seems like another lifetime. Now I sit on a board, my pale yellow peaks looking out across a dining room table to rowan trees flying in the wind and a bank of roses.

It's so peaceful here. When the next guest slices me, in cuts the pain, but lighter and lighter, until nothing remains.

Turn

Elegant terns with orange beaks and forked tails pool and rise in the shallows of the bay emitting cries millions of years old, echoed by long-beaked marbled godwits, black-bellied plover, western gulls with brown-feathered juveniles as large as themselves.

We step across the road into Owl Canyon, follow a short trail, ducking under willow and eucalyptus, crawling below lichen-layered trunks to listen to a trickling creek, and pick a few blackberries stretching past cow parsley and hemlock into the ancient mists. We laugh at our foolish notions of time—the master we're forever fleeing from in fear and disbelief, when she always in her generosity gives enough, depending on how we turn.

Hidden Under Whiteness

Pines hidden under whiteness.
Snow or early-morning fog
covering my heart?

Rooted Night

1

I see him clear—skinny-ribbed, dark
curly hair—the dried-out ditch
for a dare. He shinnies up a pine
higher, higher, under the pelting sun
until thinning limbs sway, and I worry
for him as his mother did. Yet he keeps
going and calls down in laughing peals
Hey, look at me! I can see so far!

Now to climb down. Heart pumping,
he feels for toeholds while gripping
branches so slipping feet can burrow
in a fold—a shifting, temporary home.
He jumps the last few feet and lands
on the ground—brown eyes longingly
glance back. How far I've fallen
from that child's heights!

11

But still he wings in me—love
of trees, life teeming all around,
that fecund wealth within—their quiet
power, rollicking waves of rhyme
sponged from his mother's tongue,
the grief I feel for fallen friends—
the oak, the bay—brought down
by endless, whining teeth.

A thousandfold our bodies twine
with trees, trees' spirit twinned
and breathing in our own—in sunlit
limbs, in somber silhouette,
in the spirited unseen women
and men who plumb the depths
of rooted night to water seeds
with light through open, pulsing hearts.

The Call

My sheikh is meditating—
   I feel the call
      like a church bell or a minaret
         drawing me deeper, deeper.

Whoever says *there is no*
   time is correct. Beyond
      time, beyond mind, deepest
         peace!

This ocean waiting for lovers
   to dive in.

Poems and Songs by Raphael Block,
Composed for Choir by John Maas

October Butterfly

John Maas

Pink Lillies

Poem by Raphael Block, Music by John Maas 2012

* for the last 8th note before "mer", sopranoes cross--just the one note

128

Fly Amour

(Written for Electronic Music)

Your love has wings—
it takes me to
the farthest corners
and back into myself.

It flies through mountains,
reaches into emptiness—
back into myself.

Your mirth-filled face
lights my happiness,
your sorrowing
break me into tears.

Without you, my soul's left
flapping in the wind—
all bearings lost.

Until through darkness
I have journeyed,
to find solace in your arms—

this loving Earth contains
me, my hands and feet
receive your fire.

Plunging into depths—
the sea lifts me
on wild, frothing crests—
winged horses come to rest.

Oh, Holy Lord

Raphael Block

(Written for a Gospel Choir)

V2. Help me to hear beyond the noise
help me catch your clear still voice.
Clasp me tightly to your bosom
soften me in your harmonies.

V3. Oh Holy Lord, Holy Lord
I feel your presence flame in all.
Bring me nearer to your bosom
sweeten me in your harmonies.

About the Author

Born on a kibbutz, Raphael Block spent his boyhood playing on the hills of Haifa. His family returned to London as he turned nine, where learning British English shaped his ear for sound. In 1993 he moved to Northern California with his American wife, Deborah Simon, and their three-year-old daughter, Theadora. After Deborah passed away from cancer in 2002, it became Raphael's privilege to raise their child.

Raphael was a teacher. He worked with under-fives for many years in London's inner city. In California he taught all grade levels, including teaching Waldorf, and also worked with kids with disabilities. A Sufi meditation practice, along with two life-threatening illnesses, Crohn's and MDS, a form of leukemia, have played major roles in intensifying his appreciation and gratitude for the moments of each day.

Raphael Block's poetry, infused with a perceptive love of nature, speaks to Earth's call for a heartfelt response to our ecological crisis.

www.ingramcontent.com/pod-product-compliance
Lightning Source LLC
Chambersburg PA
CBHW060355090426
42734CB00011B/2144